SUPER SCIENTISTS

DAVID ATTENBOROUGH

Sarah Ridley

W
FRANKLIN WATTS
LONDON · SYDNEY

First published in 2014 by Franklin Watts

Franklin Watts
338 Euston Road, London NW1 3BH

Franklin Watts Australia
Level 17/207 Kent Street, Sydney, NSW 2000

Editor in Chief: John C. Miles
Design: Jonathan Hair and Matt Lilly
Art Director: Peter Scoulding
Picture Research: Diana Morris
Original design concept: Sophie Williams

Picture credits: Associated Newspapers/Rex Feature: 11. Courtesy
of the Attenborough family/Mirrorpix: 4. Miles Barton/Nature PL:
21. bluehand/Shutterstock: 6. Greg Breese/US Fish and Wildlife
Service USGS: 16. David Cairns/Getty Images: 14. Richard
Carey/Dreamstime: 20. Huw Cordey/Nature Pl: 1, 2, 22. Rob
Cousins Nature PL: front cover. Ed g2s/CC/Wikipedia Commons:
7. Evantravels/Shutterstock: 15. Ben Osborne/Nature PL: 18.
Picturepoint/Topham: 10. Suzanne Plunkett/Getty Images: 23.
Popperfoto/Getty Images: 8, 12. John Sparks/Nature PL: 17. Paul
Stein JC/Creative Commons/Share Alike: 13. UPP/Topfoto: 19.
Jiri Vaclavek/Shutterstock: 5. William Vanderson/Getty Images: 9.

Dewey number: 508'.092
HB ISBN 978 1 4451 3059 0
Library eBook ISBN 978 1 4451 3066 8

Printed in China

Franklin Watts is a division of Hachette Children's Books,
an Hachette UK company.

www.hachette.co.uk

Contents

Childhood

David Attenborough was born in London in 1926. A few years later, his family moved to Leicester where his father had a new job.

John, David and Richard, the Attenborough brothers.

This fossil has been split in half to show the insides of the fossilised ammonite.

8 May 1926
David is born in London.

1928
David's younger brother, John, is born.

1931
The family moves to Leicester. His father becomes head of University College.

As a child, fossils fascinated David. He went for cycle rides into the countryside to search for them and even set up his own little museum. He loved to crack open a rock and discover a fossil of an animal that no one had seen for 150 million years or more.

5

Education and first job

1937–1944

David attends Wyggeston Grammar School, Leicester.

1944–1947

He studies for a degree in natural sciences at Clare College, Cambridge.

1947–1949

He does National Service with the navy.

1950

He marries Jane and starts his first job, as a junior editor.

Like his brothers, David went to the local grammar school. When he was fourteen, two German sisters joined the family. They had fled Germany on the *Kindertransport*.

At home, David bred tropical fish, including guppies.

6

1937–1951

David went to university at Clare College, Cambridge.

David did well at school and went on to study at Cambridge University. After his degree and two years in the navy he started a job as a junior editor of science textbooks. He also married Jane, who he'd met at university.

Starting at the BBC

1952

David starts to work for the BBC. He works on several programmes, including quiz shows.

Bored with his first job, David applied for a job working in BBC radio. He did not get the job but he was invited to train for a job in television. Soon he was making programmes, even though one boss thought his teeth were too big for a television presenter!

1954

He starts working on *Zoo Quest*.

David stands next to a BBC camera.

David and Jack Lester, a zookeeper at London Zoo, plan a trip to Guiana.

David worked on programmes about all sorts of subjects, from knitting to music. His own fascination with nature inspired him to develop a series called *Zoo Quest*. It showed experts from London Zoo collecting wild animals for the zoo.

BREAKTHROUGH

Zoo Quest was a new type of television programme. Not only did it show animals close up in the London film studio but it also showed them out in the wild.

Zoo Quest

Soon David was presenting *Zoo Quest* as well as filming it. Working on the series took him all over the world. He was amazed by the variety of animals and plants he saw and was thrilled to present them to the British people.

David shows an armadillo to the Zoo Quest *audience.*

1954

Jack Lester of London Zoo falls ill, leaving David as the presenter of *Zoo Quest*.

1954–63

David writes, presents and records the sound for *Zoo Quest*. He also writes books about his travels.

London Zoo decided to stop sending experts to the *Zoo Quest* team. This meant that David had to catch the animals himself and help look after them on the return journey.

David holds a bear cub during the filming of Zoo Quest.

EXPERIMENT

Cameras in the 1950s had clockwork parts that the cameraman had to wind up every 40 seconds. Watch a Zoo Quest programme online. Imagine the film's editor putting the programme together joining many sections of film, some with only a few seconds of useful material.

1957
The BBC Natural History Unit and the Travel and Exploration Unit are set up.

1960
David works on *Travellers' Tales*.

1961
David films Elsa, the lioness featured in the film *Born Free*.

Work and family

David with his wife, Jane, and their children, Susan and Robert.

David was away for three or four months at a time. Back at home, his wife Jane brought up their children and helped care for some of the animals David brought back from his travels.

1954–65

David made other television programmes as well as *Zoo Quest*, including a series about explorers and their travels. He became fascinated by the different ways of life of people in far away countries and made films about them when he could.

1954–63

David travels all around the world for *Zoo Quest*.

1960

He makes a series called *The People of Paradise*, about life in the South Pacific.

1962

He starts another degree, studying social anthropology. He still works part-time for the BBC.

1965

He makes a series about the Zambezi river in Africa.

The film crew filmed the land-diving ceremony on Pentecost Island, Vanuatu in the South Pacific.

13

A desk job

David sat at a desk and worked in an office for his new job but he still made a few films.

In 1965, David was offered an important job in charge of the newly formed BBC2 channel. Although he had started a new university course, he decided to take the job and return to the BBC full-time.

1965

David becomes controller of BBC2. He is responsible for some brilliant series.

1967

He is in charge of bringing in colour television broadcasting.

Now David led a team of people who decided which programmes to make and when to show them on television. Two years later he was also in charge of bringing in colour television. This was not an easy job since most people still owned black-and-white TV sets.

These men from Bali are playing in a group of instruments called a gamelan. David included gamelan music in a 1969 film about Bali.

1969

He becomes director of BBC1 and 2.

1969

He works on *The Miracle of Bali*.

1973

David decides to return to wildlife films.

Life on Earth

1973

David writes and presents *Eastwards with Attenborough*.

In 1973, David returned to making films. Soon he was working on *Life on Earth*, a series about how life developed on Earth. It was watched by about 500 million people across the world.

1974/75

He writes and presents *Tribal Eye*, about tribal art.

1976–79

He writes and presents *Life on Earth* and writes a book that becomes a bestseller.

One episode of Life on Earth *included the moment when millions of horseshoe crabs come out of the water to lay their eggs.*

1973–1980

Filming brought David into close contact with mountain gorillas.

It took David and his team three years to write, film and present *Life on Earth*. He loved being able to watch and film beautiful animals all around the world.

BREAKTHROUGH

Many people think that the *Life on Earth* series changed the way people watched television. Viewers were gripped by the 13 episodes, shown week after week.

Wildlife galore

Soon he was making two more big television series. *The Living Planet* is about the natural world and *The Trials of Life* is about animal behaviour. Film cameras had become so good that David and the film crew were now able to film animals wherever and however they wanted.

This picture shows David filming an episode of Life in the Freezer *in the Antarctic.*

1984

The Living Planet is watched on television.

1985

David becomes Sir David Attenborough.

1990

The Trials of Life is watched on television.

1980s–1990s

As well as the big television series, David worked on other smaller series about plants and each of the animal groups. Since plants grow slowly, David and his team set up cameras and then speeded up the film, to great effect.

David with a titan arum, a huge plant that flowers once every 1,000 days.

1993	**1995–96**	**1997**	**1998**
David works on *Life in the Freezer*, about the wildlife of Antarctica.	He works on *The Private Life of Plants*.	Jane, his wife, falls ill and dies.	*Life of Birds* is shown on television.

David as narrator

While he was writing and filming his own television series, David also narrated many others, from *Wildlife on One* to *The Blue Planet* and *Planet Earth*. As a narrator, he spoke the words that were heard with the films but he was not filmed in the wild.

The Blue Planet *looked at life in seas and oceans all across the world.*

2001	2002	2005	2006
David narrates *The Blue Planet*.	*The Life of Mammals* is shown on television. David is voted one of the '100 Greatest Britons'.	*Life in the Undergrowth* explores the world of insects and invertebrates. Elizabeth II awards David the Order of Merit.	David narrates *Planet Earth*.

1990s–2011

David with an Oustalet's chameleon in Life in Cold Blood.

Life in Cold Blood completed David's work on the animal kingdom. In *Frozen Planet* David was the narrator but he wrote the final episode and spoke out about the impact of climate change on the Arctic and Antarctic.

2007	2008	2009	2010	2011
He makes two films about climate change and its causes.	*Life in Cold Blood* focuses on reptiles and amphibians.	He presents programmes about Charles Darwin.	He presents the latest research about fossils.	*Frozen Planet* is shown on TV.

Protecting plant Earth

2009/11

David writes and
records 40 short
radio programmes
called *Life Stories*.

2012

He works with
3D cameras to
make films for Sky
Television.

2012

His life is
celebrated in the
TV series: *60 Years
in the Wild* and
Attenborough's Ark.

2012/13

He writes and
presents *Africa*.

David has won countless awards for
his work and continues to work on
programmes and write books. He uses
his fame to reach people in power and
asks them to take action against climate
change and to control world population.

*David has returned to Africa many times. This photo
with a meerkat was taken in 2000.*

Wearing 3D glasses, David (second from right) and guests including the Duke and Duchess of Cambridge watch his film that brings extinct animals to life at the Natural History Museum, London, on 11 December 2013.

David brings his own wonder about the natural world into people's homes through their television screens. He hopes the programmes he makes will make people care about and protect our fragile Earth and its wildlife.

Glossary

ammonite An ancient animal that lived in the sea.

climate change A change in world climate, the usual weather and temperature of a place, particularly in the past 50 years.

degree Three- or four-year course at university.

editor Someone whose work makes books ready to be published.

environmentalist Someone who is particularly concerned about protecting the natural world.

fossil The trace of an ancient animal or plant in a rock.

grammar school A selective school.

horseshoe crab A type of crab, with ancestors dating back 150 million years.

kindertransport The rescue operation that brought 10,000 Jewish children from Germany and Austria to Britain before the Second World War.

land-diving ceremony Teenage boys on Pentecost Island jump off a tall structure with vines attached to their ankles – like bungee jumping.

national service Between 1949 and 1963, all men between the ages of 17 and 21 had to spend at least 18 months in the armed forces.

natural sciences All the sciences: biology, chemistry and physics.

social anthropology The study of how people live, what they believe and how they live together.

television series A group of television programmes that are linked together and focus on the same or similar subjects.

3D Three dimensional

Index